THE GREAT Ladybird 50th BIRTHDAY competition book

illustrated by PETER STEVENSON

Ladybird Books

**FOR ENTRY
FORM AND PRIZE
DETAILS TURN TO
BACK PAGES**

Out of the window went the seeds,
They grew up overnight.
Out of the little bed jumped the girl
And disappeared from sight.

①

Over the bridge they had to go
To eat grass that was juicy and green.
Seventeen minus ten gives the number
    of men
With a princess to keep their house
    clean.

(2)

This little girl walked alone in the forest,
To take her poor granny some cake.
When the witch looked into the oven,
They pushed her inside it to bake.

3

Three brothers built three houses
But now there's only one.
This man left his work one night;
By morning it was done.

④

*F*ive add on two, and then take away
    four,
They went for a walk and did not
    lock their door.
Seven plus eight, then take away
    three,
Gives the number of clock chimes
    in this mystery.

(5)

Deep in the woods was a house
   so sweet,
Two little children thought it
   a treat.
Deep into sleep a fair princess fell,
Caught in the trap of a wicked spell.

6

Marry my son, Mother Toad said;
Come live with us and stay.
Nobody loved this little bird,
He hid himself away.

⑦

*W*ith a beautiful comb entwined in her hair,
She lay on the floor as if dead.
When a girl went to Granny's one fine sunny day,
She found someone else there instead!

(8)

What a lot of work is done
At night in this small shop.
What a lot of huff and puff
To make two houses flop.

(9)

This four-legged creature,
  who likes catching mice,
Is dressed like the smartest of men.
But I'm RED, and my first is in HOUSE,
  not in MOUSE,
My second and third are in TEN.

(10)

Time stood still in the castle,
Nothing quivered and all seemed dead.
When the stranger wasn't paid,
He took the boys and girls instead.

*T*wo lizards changed into footmen,
Then back into lizards again,
A boy climbed up high,
   to a place in the sky
And returned with a magical hen.

⑫

WIN *A FANTASTIC HOLIDAY TO ORLANDO, FLORIDA – the sunshine state of America and home of*

Walt Disney World®

© The Walt Disney Company

LADYBIRD BOOKS LTD offers a chance of a lifetime seven-day holiday for you and your family with *Virgin* holidays.

TURN TO BACK PAGE FOR MORE DETAILS

ENTRY FORM

To enter **The Great Ladybird 50th Birthday Competition** complete the entry details below, and write the names of the hidden picture clues and mystery fairytales into the answer grid on the next page. Then return this form to:

The Great Ladybird 50th Birthday Competition, Ladybird Books Ltd, Beeches Road, Loughborough, Leicestershire LE11 2NQ, to arrive by Monday 31st December 1990.

Name_____ Age_____

Address_____

_____

_____

_____ Post code_____

Signature of parent or guardian _____

Number of hidden ladybirds

Complete the following sentence
in not more than twenty words:

My favourite fairytale is _____

because _____

_____

_____

_____

HIDDEN PICTURE CLUE

MYSTERY FAIRYTALE

1	
2	
3	
4	
5	
6	
7	
8	
9	
10	
11	
12	

Rules of the competition

1. The competition is open to all children resident in United Kingdom, Eire and Japan only who are 10 years old or under at 31st December 1990.
2. The completed entry form must be returned to Ladybird Books Ltd and arrive by 31st December 1990.
3. Any entries which have been filled in incorrectly will be disqualified.
4. Persons not eligible to enter the competition are:
   (a) Any employee of Ladybird Books Ltd or its subsidiary companies (b) Any employee of Virgin Atlantic Airways (c) Any employee of Virgin Holidays Ltd (d) Any employee of the Quality Inn Hotel (e) A judge of the competition (f) Any immediate family of the above.
5. The competition will be judged by a Guest Celebrity.
6. The winning entry will be the first all-correct competition form drawn from all those received by the closing date.
7. The winner will be notified by post during the week commencing Monday 4th February 1991.
8. The judges' decision is final and no correspondence will be entered into.
9. No cash alternatives will be offered.
10. The holiday for a family of four (two adults and two children) can be taken at any time during 1991, subject to availability.
11. If you wish to be notified of the winner, please enclose a stamped addressed envelope with your entry.
12. By entering the competition all competitors will be deemed to have agreed to abide by the rules of the competition.